A Leaf

Story by Johnny Ray Moore
Illustrations by Kristin Rauchenstein

A leaf fell from the tree onto the porch.

It caused the sleeping cat to knock over a bucket that rolled down the steps.

The bucket rolled out in front of a boy riding a skateboard.

The boy crashed
into a hot dog stand.
The hot dogs went rolling
along the sidewalk.

**The dogs began chasing the hot dogs.
They frightened a squirrel that was jumping from tree to tree.**

Then one more leaf fell onto the porch...

just when the cat was going to sleep, once again.

LOVE ME WHEN I'M MOST UNLOVABLE

BOOK TWO: THE KIDS' VIEW

Poetry and Prose by
Robert Ricken

National Association of Secondary School Principals

Contributing Authors:

**Kristen Cossaart
Michael Elston
Dolores Fernandez
Blanca Garcia
Veronica Hernandez
Diane Hurley
Beth Kantrowitz
Cynthia Lozano
Patricia Nilales
Katie Reichenberger
Julie Schuster
Laurie Schuster**

Dedicated to my wife, Susan

Special thanks to

Ann Farrell *Laura Kwiatek* *Dorothy Szigethy*

© 1987

National Association of Secondary School Principals
1904 Association Dr., Reston, Va. 22091

ISBN 0-882-10198-6